Playing Poker With
Tennessee Williams

www.blacklawrence.com

Executive Editor: Diane Goettel
Book and Cover Design: Zoe Norvell
Cover Art: "Big Red Doors in the French Quarter" by Diane Millsap

Copyright © Kevin Pilkington 2021
ISBN: 978-1-62557-834-1

Published 2021 by Black Lawrence Press.
Printed in the United States.

Playing Poker With Tennessee Williams

Kevin Pilkington

Black Lawrence Press

For Celia, now more than ever.

"He stands before a tree. Within the tree is
a word that becomes a name."

— Patti Smith

"I took my power in my hand
And went against the world;"

— Emily Dickinson

Acknowledgments

Grateful acknowledgment is made to the editors of the following publications where these poems first appeared:

Academy of American Poets Poem-A-Day/Poets.org: *Pomegranate*

Catamaran: *A Church on the Edge of the Bed*

Exit 13: *Bob's Tavern: The Worst Food and the Coldest Beer in Colorado, Taking Risks*

Illuminating Faith Anthology, New York Quarterly Books: *Lights*

Inkwell: *August 3:00 AM, Cake, Elephants*

Lumina: *Imagination*

New York Quarterly: *Elegy for Art, Stan Getz in the Refrigerator*

Paterson Literary Review: *Completely Dry, Old Men*

Streetlight Magazine: *Peace Offering, Bridges*

Valparaiso Review: *Mingus*

Table of Contents

III.

I.

Teach me mortality,
frighten me into the present.

— Jack Gilbert

Pomegranate

A woman walks by the bench I'm sitting on
with her dog that looks part Lab, part Buick,
stops and asks if I would like to dance.
I smile, tell her of course I do. We decide
on a waltz that she begins to hum.

We spin and sway across the street in between
parked cars and I can tell she realizes
she chose a man who understands the rhythm
of sand, the boundaries of thought. We glide
and Fred and Ginger might come to mind or
a breeze filled with the scent of flowers of your choice.
Coffee stops flowing as a waitress stares out the window
of a diner while I lead my partner back across the street.

When we come to the end of our dance,
we compliment each other and to repay the favor
I tell her to be careful since the world comes to an end
three blocks to the east of where we stand. Then
I remind her as long as there is a '59 Cadillac parked
somewhere in a backyard between here and Boise
she will dance again.

As she leaves content with her dog, its tail wagging
like gossip, I am convinced now more than ever
that I once held hundreds of roses in my hands
the first time I cut open a pomegranate.

Other Modes of Transportation

Last week an old tenement three over
from ours caught fire. The flames
may have been on a crash diet
the way they burned through each
floor as if they were calories.

Yesterday a construction crew began
drilling a hole in the street right
outside our building. Although it
is deep they still have miles to go
if they plan on reaching China.

Things are getting better though.
The birds on the ledge outside our
bedroom window every morning
sound more like Paul Desmond's sax
and I upgraded my smartphone
to a genius.

I've also found I make a lot less
mistakes whenever I'm late for the train.
The only trips worth taking are like
this one, sitting here with you, talking
and every once in a while simply gaze
at your shoulders and travel the length
of your hair.

A Church on the Edge of the Bed

There was a fire in the church
uptown near the tracks that destroyed
everything except for a shell of walls
and a few prayers that floated
away now that the roof is sky.

Passing by it on the train
reminded me how it looked
a lot like Billie Holiday's voice
on her last album.

I had to turn away
when it began to resemble
my father sitting on the edge
of his bed, after the stroke, alone
for the first time, hanging on
after years of stone and wood,
out of prayers and waiting for no one.

Bridges

I'm on the roof deck of a building
45 stories high that aren't all worth
reading. This is the only place I can
stay above it all and by the time the noise
on the street reaches this height it turns
into Mozart. The sky is clear except
for a cloud a helicopter rips into shreds
with its blades. Queens looks like braille
I can rub my fingers over in case I want
to see even more. The East River lets another
ship slide by and I wonder if we are related
since I have been sliding by for years.
All the bridges can fit on the table
of the model train set my brother and I
had as kids. No wonder the freight train
going over Hell Gate looks Lionel and Wards
Island Bridge is small enough to pin on my lapel.

I walk over to look downtown, past the new
apartment building three blocks away that is all
glass, chrome and resembles Cary Grant.
Just below 2nd Ave. there is a park the size
of a green mat. I'd like to pick it up and place in front
of my door so anyone who stops by can wipe
their shoes on treetops. The Empire State always
reminds me of a syringe a doctor is holding up
waiting for me to pull down my pants. And further
back where the sky is torn and ripped

the World Trade Towers stood. There are new
buildings under construction all over and a flock
of giant birds who flew out of those Japanese monster movies
from the sixties nest on top of them like cranes.

This is a city that keeps changing, where block parties
are a new religion, dogs walk their owners, guys still
leave bars and piss between parked cars until their bladders
turn to sand, winters bring snow and ice and the police bring
heat. No one gets along, but everyone else does. There's no
denying in back of me Billie Holiday died in Metropolitan
Hospital tied to her bed. This, however, is what I'm certain
of—somewhere down there a woman is waiting just for me
who smells like flowers.

August 3:00 AM

The noise on the street got me out
of bed and over to the window.
I opened the blinds and for a few
seconds the empty tenement three over
looked like my cousin back from
the bars on 3rd with flames shooting
out of his head. Then I blinked my eyes
clear and saw it was even worse—
the entire building was on fire, flames
sticking out of the roof and front
windows, licking the breeze trying to set
it on fire too.

Both ends of the block were closed
off and fire trucks and an ambulance
were parked in the middle of the heatwave,
lights blinking as if something was caught
in their beams. Police roped off a crowd
who gathered to watch as if celebrities,
Brad Pitt or Beyoncé, would come out
of the building with their careers on fire
and stop to pose for selfies. Sparks shot
up from the roof like stars you
have to travel two hours north of the city
to find or the glitter in Alia and Connie,
names pinned to waitress uniforms in
the diner around the block.

By dawn, the firemen put the flames
out but the building was still smoking
like it had a three-pack-a-day habit.
I was sweating, relieved the fire hadn't spread,
then turned the A/C all the way up and fell back
on the bed with the cold air blowing on me.
I turned into a chunk of ice large enough
to keep every bottle of beer cold at an end
of summer block party. Relieved and exhausted,
I fell back to sleep, my eyes frozen shut.

Trumpets and Candles

I stand in back of the church
near the entrance. It's dark
and empty except for a guy sleeping
it off in the first pew, curled
on his side like an S who must
have tied one on and fallen off
the alphabet.

There is a large crucifix in back
of the altar. From where I stand
Jesus looks like he just got back
from the gym and is strong enough
to pull those nails out by himself
if he wanted.

Just to be clear, I'm the kind
who doesn't believe in much
and this is a stop I thought I'd never
make. It's just that I'm looking
for a miracle the doctors say my cousin
needs to walk out of Sloan-Kettering.

I look around at the statues
walk over to the nearest one who
has no name on the plaque under her feet.
She is gazing down at me and I
think her smile is sexy, seductive
and how those kinds of thoughts

won't help so I look at the candles
next to her.

The ones that are lit flicker
and move like the kids who
breakdance on 5th Avenue during
the holidays for the hat money
from the crowds who surround them.
I watch too, put change in the donation
box like it's a slot machine and hope
the candle I light has three apples
lined in a row in it instead of wax.

I kneel in front of the statue
but can't remember any prayers
with marble or even with any stone
less expensive, clasp my hands
together and rest my lips against
them as if they are a trumpet.

I close my eyes making sure every word
is pitch-perfect, my cousin needs that miracle,
every word the right musical note.
I'm fucking Harry James, blowing
prayers through my horn,
pointing it up at the ceiling
and loud enough to wake every
goddamn angel who might be sleeping.

Open Heart

A few tenements and rooftops
is the entire world that fits in
my window. In this cold, smoke
coming out of chimneys looks
like whipped cream and even if
you are single it doesn't matter
since the snow that fell last
night covered the entire city
like a wedding dress—tomorrow
traffic will stain it black and gray.
A plow passes by scraping the street
the way I used to scrape by for years.
Heat coming out of the radiators
below it is warm creating the kind
of relationship I always knew
one day I was capable of having.
In this kind of weather birds go
missing, making it easier to
see the surgeon walk towards me
after the operation, saying he held
my father's heart in his hands
to check if there was any more damage.
No matter what I have done,
I become a surgeon too, every time
I think of my father and how
I hold his heart gently in my
hands, as I am doing now,
at this very moment, 20 years later.

Andy Warhol's Wig

I'm on the balcony of a condo in
Las Olas on the twenty-fifth floor
that seems even higher, but nothing
can get this boring party off the ground.
A pool next door from here looks
no bigger than a postcard with green
water that seems dry enough to write
wish you were here, place a stamp
in the corner where a tube floats
then stick it in the mail. The sky
is clear except for a cloud that must be
covered in seventy-five sunblock to stay
so white and keep from getting burned.
A freighter coming into port with boxes
and crates looking like tenements from home
or at least an entire block from Brooklyn
that's arriving for vacation. Sometimes
the wind takes knots out of my hair,
at other times I can lean on it the way
my last wife could never lean on me. Gulls
won't let me forget the East River and what keeps
me awake at home helps me sleep down here.

I think about leaving, but at this height I can brag
that for a few hours I was able to stay on top
of things. When it gets so hot even locals begin
to melt, I notice another cloud the color
of Andy Warhol's wig heading towards South Beach

and it's the only chance I have to impress
a woman sipping a glass of wine near the door.
So, I stand on a chair, get up on my toes, reach
and slide it over the sun to cool things down.
Then I turn to look at her with the type of smile
on my face that can't hide the fact that I'm
the kind of man who hasn't done much with my life
up until just now, but she already went back inside.
I decide it's time to leave and notice a beach ball
near her chair. It looks a lot like a globe as I pick
it up, spin it in my hands, stop on Africa, with my thumb and
index finger resting on Europe. It reminds
me how I hate to fly. So instead of getting up to catch
a flight back to New York in the morning, I stick
my thumbs into Canada, rip it open like a peach,
bite into the world letting the Atlantic drip down
my chin and onto my shirt, then eat my way home.

Dieting

I've been on a diet for over a week and work out
every day. I was in the gym on the stationary
bike this morning, placed a novel in front
of me and began to pedal through it. Took only
forty minutes to get from Bull Run to Gettysburg
without getting shot then had to stop when the woman
next to me told her friend she was hungry to start
a new project at work and I kept wondering
what did they serve it with?

Later I walked over to the post office and passed
a guy walking a hound shaped like a hot dog
that was cute but would look even better with mustard
spread over it from head to tail. A few blocks later, I
noticed a thin layer of snow covering a small garden on
the side of a brownstone making the bushes and kale
vegetables waiting to be served on a white platter.
The smell coming out of the bakery on Second
added a lot more calories to every breeze; to play it
safe I held my breath and crossed the street.

I stopped in a deli to get a cup of coffee and stared
at their pastry shaped like small wheels reminding
me to hurry up and roll out of there. After mailing my
package, I walked down the street steep as a hill
that is blocked off from traffic and where kids slide down
on tires shaped like the donuts I just walked away from.
Still, I wondered if I took one and dunked it in my coffee

how would it taste. When I got home and she
came out of the bedroom in a new short black dress
bought on sale, of course, she wanted to know how
it looked. I stared for a moment and said, *good enough
to eat.*

Old Men

Old men turn white,
creak when they walk,
lose jobs, teeth and keep
their eyes in water. Young
girls and boys are countries
they can never travel to again.
They tell stories no one listens
to. Snails move faster.

They are the lucky ones though,
knowing everything you don't.
Why boxing rings are square
instead of round, that all angels
are black and sound like Louie
Armstrong's trumpet.

If you feel like you are running
out of time, they are not.
They will just tell you any decade
is worth it and is always better
grilled with a glass of wine.

You can find them in any
park waiting on a bench.
All you have to do is ask.
All you have to do is listen.

Not Asking for Much

I want it growling like a wolf
as it runs towards me before it lunges,
Godzilla stomping, each footfall an earthquake
as it moves up First Avenue, a spaceship
shaped like a large plate in the middle
of a dinner table with enough food in it
to feed a family of five, spinning a strange
sound before it lands in Central Park.
I need noise that will give me enough time
to run and get away. Instead this virus is
the Invisible Man, Claude Rains, walking silently.
I have no idea when it attacks.

And there is no special ray gun, or sword
that lights up when lifted in both hands.
Instead—the weapon isn't designed by Spielberg—
it turns out to be a bar of soap. That's right the bar
of soap that rests in a dish near my toothbrush.
It can't kill the virus except for the germs
growing in it. And we all have to stay at least
six feet away from strangers to help stop
the spread. I like to stay as far away
as my ex-wife but not as far as my last girlfriend.

A hotspot used to mean a trendy restaurant
downtown where I could never get a table.
Now the entire city is a hotspot where there
are no empty beds in any hospital that is filled

with the sick and dying. New York, this has got
to stop. I want you back the way you were.

I want subways to rattle and shake
the fear out of me; trains to leave Grand Central
and come back the exact same way; empty
streets crowded again with people whose
faces are countries I have never been to and
all the laughing and talking, blending together
sounding like the globe. It's not asking
too much. I don't want to wear a mask
anymore as if I'm riding with the James
Gang on our way to rob a Chase Bank.
I want to be able to sneeze and not be afraid
I killed someone.

At least I still believe in the leaves
on the tree outside my apartment building.
They will soon look like they were dipped in
cream for two weeks before blowing away
and are the first signs of spring every year.
Come on New York, I am not asking for much.
I would give anything, really, just about anything
if I could simply walk up to you and shake your hand.

II.

Pretend you don't owe me a thing
And maybe we'll roll out of here

— Ai

Cake

I stopped at a friend's
apartment who was baking
a cake. She had the recipe
opened on the counter next
to a script of a play she
was cast in, memorizing lines
in between flour and sugar.
She invited me back for dinner
that night.

The wine, a rosé,
tasted like spring and we drank
until April was empty.
For dessert, she brought out
the cake and cut a large piece
that sat on my plate like
the Flatiron building.

She warned me it might taste
a bit unusual since she mixed
the recipe with some of the play's
dialogue by mistake. I was
full but it tasted wealthy,
not rich so I could take a few
extra bites even though they tasted
more and more like the first act.

Stan Getz in the Refrigerator

The heatwave has been breaking
records all week so to play it safe
I keep my vinyl jazz albums in
the refrigerator. Miles Davis is behind
the milk, Stan Getz near the butter.
My apartment is cool enough for now
with the A/C set on a temperature
somewhere between my two ex-wives
and a brother I haven't seen in years.

I look out the window and notice
a woman standing alone at the corner
in high heels holding an umbrella
the size of a dinner plate over her head.
Even though I can't see her face
I recognize her since she still dresses
all in red. Either I once slept
with her, or she once slept with me.

There's a traffic jam on First Avenue
with yellow cabs stuck in it
like half a dozen eggs and just another way
the city stays hungry. It must
be the construction a few blocks
north causing the backup. I can see
a cloud got caught on the long arm
of a crane that now looks dry, out of water
and hangs from it like a white rag.

A firetruck tries making its way
uptown through the traffic, each car
crawling out of the way and almost
mounting the car in front of it like
animals on Wild Kingdom. The siren
gets louder as it gets closer, reminding
me how I was once on fire when I first
moved here, a blaze no one could put out.

First Avenue, like every other street in the city,
has become a skillet. Those cabs are now an omelet,
the sidewalks strips of bacon and it all
goes with a side of toast. That's why I'm
just trying to keep my place cool. In
a couple of minutes, it will be
cool as Sinatra backed up by the Basie
band in front of a sold-out room at
the Sands. That's how cool I want it,
even if it means bringing 1966 all the way
back around again.

Lights

I don't like looking at lights
on lower Broadway. Some stare
others blink reminding me of the lights
on the machines in the back of my
father's hospital bed that last night.
I stood near his feet, my mother
at his side holding his hand looking
into his closed eyes saying to both of us
they had been through a lot over the past
forty years and they would get through
this too. I knew he wouldn't get through
the night but there wasn't any way of knowing
my mother was sick. She said nothing until
a week after my father was gone.

Waiting on the corner of 23rd Street
for the light to change, I'm at the side of her bed
two months after my father was buried, lights
blinking in back of her this time. Her eyes are closed
and I'm thinking how all the prayers she said
over the years, all the churches she entered,
the rows and rows of candles she lit, enough to set
the entire East Coast on fire, all the beads she pressed between
her fingers from the rosaries she carried
in her coat pockets could do nothing, absolutely nothing
to stop tumors the size of a baby's fist from growing
in her stomach.

As I make my way over to York Avenue
to catch the first bus home, I stop walking to watch
a white ship on the East River that looks like an angel
on a break, and on its back floating downtown
towards the harbor.

The Promise of Water

I'm standing on a bluff
overlooking the Caribbean—
two buildings from across the cove
shine their lights,
long golden bars resting
on the surface of the water.
They are shaped like the Twin
Towers, reminding me how
life was and how it can never
be again.

Further out a cruise ship
is anchored glittering
like a diamond bracelet
that slides off the expensive wrist
of a woman on her way to a banquet.
If I still believed in Christ
I would walk out and take it
then jog back if the waves
were thick enough to hold me up.

I'd then book the next flight to New York,
sitting with the bracelet locked
in a case on my lap until we landed.
Then I'd hurry home, wrap it around
your wrist and watch as your eyes fill
with stars.

Completely Dry

The day after she moved out
I went for a walk and stopped
next to the only tree growing
in front of the tenements across
from mine. It's about four stories high
but not yet a novel. Birds fly up
and down its trunk like Coltrane's
fingers on his sax. I appreciate it
being there and listen to the songs
it plays since I could always carry
a lot of guilt but never a tune.
Even in the shower if I try to sing
I sound like a crowded sidewalk
in a rainstorm.

I don't want to go back to my
apartment yet. If I keep the windows
open anyone can hear how empty
it sounds. It doesn't even have an old
dog curled into a tire sleeping under
the table that I can wake and roll
outside instead of making him walk.
Or a goldfish staring at me from his bowl
wondering how I can get through
life completely dry.

Now I wanted the tree to play one
of those old standards by Mercer

or Van Heusen, something soft with
a melody that sounds like a bandage.
It started playing an original I had
never heard before with nothing more
than a few wings and a branch or two.
It was a tune even I could hum.
And that's when I began sobbing, not
caring how many cars passed
or who saw me. I just stood there
looking down, staring at nothing.

At the Other End of the Hall

I learned a lot about hunger
early on. It was the way cancer
ate, always starving, feeding on
my grandmother in the bedroom
down the hall from mine. It was the last
month and the only time she lived
with us. I was eight and whenever
she moaned and groaned out loud,
I knew it was feeding, gnawing
on everything it could get its tumors
on until the night I heard nothing.
So I walked down the hallway that stretched
like taffy and slowly opened her door.
The bed she was in looked big as a ship.
Her arms were thin white bones lying
across her chest—a pirate flag resting
against the pillow. And she was staring
the way a novel does that no one will ever open,
no one will ever read again.

Imagination

You said you would be home from work
early and wait for me to have dinner.
We live in a city that isn't always safe
the way Doris Day is in all those old movies.
It's a city where anything can happen
and the extra bolts on our door are another way
to prove it. So after I open the door
with the light on in the kitchen and say
I'm home like I'm holding onto a winning
lottery ticket and you don't answer, I drop
my bag as if disregarding my arm I don't
need since I have another and call your name
again. When you still don't answer, I begin
to panic, rush into the bedroom to see
if you slipped and hit your head on the floor
and start wondering how do I ever get through
one day without you in it. I'm just a man
with an imagination as wild as a Twilight
Zone Marathon. If you'd only just walk through
the door I'd give you anything—one of those
cars you like that is small enough to wrap
your arms around and hug or a bigger apartment
with enough space to fit in stars and planets
if you want. I'd give anything, anything.
When I hear keys at the door, I hurry over
to pull it open. It's you, envelopes in
your hand, saying *I just went downstairs
to get the mail.*

Upside Down

I had driven most of the night
with the windows down
and the radio up, singing along
to songs I knew and creating
lyrics to the ones I didn't.
I was making good time until
the hole in my stomach made me
look for breakfast. I got off
at the next exit and stopped in
a town somewhere between
Dylan and Springsteen.

Main Street was as long as
the comb in my hip pocket.
I parked, got out, stretched
and saw the shops were closed
except for a diner next to a butcher
shop with its sign saying *we
sell and buy game*. I had a feeling
that if a friend of mine who is a vegan
was with me the locals would think
he was an alien from a planet
that looks like a radish if seen
through a telescope.

The diner was empty except
for a guy with his back to me
at a table in one of those black and

red plaid shirts you can play
checkers on.

I took a seat at the counter near
muffins the size of softballs
and was hungry enough to take a swing
at. On the skillet were hash browns
piled up like stones after a wall
collapses and above them near
the glasses was an ad for Chesterfield
cigarettes from the 50s with its history
of lungs and lives gone up in smoke.

A waitress came in from a back room
smiling with hair the color of cold beer
asking what'll I have. I ordered the last
five days back and over easy. She pointed
to the specials on the wall. It would make
more sense to get the entire week for an
extra two bucks that came with a side of bacon.

When I got back in the car full on all
but a slice of Sunday afternoon I couldn't
finish, I felt a lot better and drove down
Main Street, with tiny specks glittering
in the tar from the sun. I realized then
that if the world at that very moment
was turned upside down, I'd be driving
across the sky over midnight towards
the highway, stars crunching
under my tires.

The Next King of Scotland

My aunt who is in her nineties
somehow never forgets my birthday.
Every December 6th a card arrives in my
mailbox on its back buried under bills
and ads for everything I'll never buy.
It's always a Hallmark card with sweet
sticky rhymes that I dunk in my coffee
before adding milk.

When I visited her last month, she wanted
to know when will I become the next
King of Scotland or better yet a fireman.
I didn't bother explaining there isn't any
nobility in our family unless we count
her husband who was a royal pain in the ass.
The hook and ladder thing might have made me
smile if it wasn't for all the fires I put out lately.

Her face is covered in wrinkles like a dress
that has spent too much time in a suitcase
and hair, the color of Miami, is pulled into a tire
resting against the back of her head. When she smiles
her wet eyes shine like lights at the bottom
of a swimming pool. If I spend too much time
with her, I always discover my mother's face,
her younger sister, and resent my aunt for living
30 years longer. It has something to do with me
punching my brother when we were kids every time

he called me a momma's boy then punching him again
because it was true.

This is where I should mention the woman I love
was in Tucson and her plane lands today in about
an hour. It's also the first day of spring and the birds
chirping outside trick me for a second into thinking
it's my cell phone. Maybe I should pick it up anyway
and listen since I might learn something more about flight.

Mingus

I take taxis just to get somewhere
learning foreign languages the drivers
speak. My Spanish has gotten stronger,
Arabic gets stuck in my throat, German
goes great with sauerkraut and I still get by
on the English I've been practicing for years.

I once saw a fisherman on the docks
beat his catch with a club. Sometimes
the city is a fisherman with a club
in its hand and I'm the one who catches
a beating. At other times the entire city
gleams like the gold chains around the necks
of guys who tunnel and bridge in on Saturday nights.

The sound of sirens is how the neighborhood
tightens its belt, and the oil cooking in fast
food joints and diners make things easier
whenever I need to slide through another day.
The best bars are at the end of my block on Second
where I can drink until I'm Jesus and cure
the leper I find in the mirror.

The few good jazz clubs are gone now,
although I can hear wind improvise
rather than gust along the street. And those
horn arrangements? Forget it. They are nothing
more than traffic in rush hour. Even though

it sounds like Mingus, it never is no matter
how much I want it to be.

Bread

There is a large bakery off First Avenue
that makes bread each day around
5:00 pm—you can smell it for blocks.
When a warm breeze passes by filled
with whole wheat or sourdough rip
a piece off to spread on some butter or traffic
jam from rush hour and let it melt.

If this makes you smile let me finish.
Last night my neighbor in his late eighties
was walking past the bakery, leaning on his cane
the way he used to lean on his wife and was stabbed
by two guys in their teens for the five-dollar bill
in his wallet. Caught a few hours later—
they were smiling too.

Gary Indiana

He was a salesman who lived
in Indiana and traveled out
of state to sell insurance in his new
DeSoto with its fins that could make
sharks jealous. When he traveled
overnight he'd try to find good coffee
shops and Sinatra on the radio
whom he loved but had to admit
there was something to that Elvis
thing. Life was good with his wife
who was starting to show
in their small comfortable home
as white as any of his favorite hymns
in a town that moved slow as cows.
He was young, in good health and never
thought about his bowels that were
just something to move until
it first happened in Davenport
where they shut down no matter
how many cups of coffee he drank
after breakfast, nothing moved
and his stomach felt like it was
filled with cement. And it stayed
that way, bloated and uncomfortable
until he got back home and everything
moved smoothly again. And that's
how it went; when he traveled
on business to another city he was

all bloat and concrete as if he
swallowed sidewalks. Then
sitting in a stall in Cedar Rapids
along with the heavy dinner from
the night before stuck in his stomach
the song Gary Indiana popped into
his head and got stuck there too
until his stomach rumbled and
he went staying there for awhile,
relieved. Two days later in Sioux City,
Iowa in his motel bathroom and needing
help he started humming the song
and once again he was moved, it wasn't
a coincidence. From then on, the song
became another kind of insurance—
every morning in Fort Wayne, Topeka
Kansas, Sioux Falls, South Dakota, Butte
Montana he hummed Gary Indiana.
When his company opened an office
in town and he no longer had to travel
he never needed to hum that tune again.

Bob's Tavern: The Worst Food and Coldest Beer in Colorado

It's what the neon sign blinked on the tavern's
roof as I pulled into the parking lot. I spent
the last few hours driving through a valley
that was wide open like a boxer who never
keeps his guard up. The last mountain peak
I passed reminded me of a shark fin, a hammerhead
on its way to take a bite out of a hill. And it takes
some getting used to, the air that is way too thin
and needs to put on weight for me to breathe
easier. It's not just me having difficulty
breathing; I passed a stream, a local that had been
here for years, that stopped running and ended up
walking in this high altitude.

The sign was right—the beer really was cold
with the kind of foam found on waves
or any ocean worth its weight in water.
Each glass was more in love with my throat
than the last—they kept losing their heads
over my thirst. And after I tried cutting into
a steak, I ordered another to bring back home
to New York and have the shoemaker on First
Avenue make them into sandals. It's been hot
and will be a lot cooler walking around
the city on sirloin.

Elegy for Art

To get out of the heat, I stopped
in a pub for a cold drink before
catching the next bus across town.
It was crowded with a party
for a guy in a photo on a table
in the center of the room. A couple
near the door were talking music
and an old man with hair the color
of cigar smoke turned to me and
said how much he loved classical
music and he wondered if I listened
to real music, the classics. I old
him of course: Sgt. Pepper, The White
Album, Beggar's Banquet were the classics
I always listen to. Sometimes that's all
it takes to make someone smile
even if you mean it.

I started to make my way over to the bar
past a small group talking politics
a topic I always avoid even though
I'm an expert on the cold war
that took place in my apartment
when I lived with my ex.
I sat next to a woman who turned
to look at me, she said nothing and let
her drink do all the talking. I looked
to her like the kind of guy

who didn't believe in god.
I answered I could never be an atheist
since they never have holidays.
Then she tried again—
I looked like the type who never
went to church. Then I'm your man
I told her after I took a hit on a cold beer
I ordered, since every priest I knew
talked about saving my soul when
they did nothing about saving Motown
that has all the soul anyone could need.
All you have to do is listen.

I turned around for a few moments as friends
took turns talking about Art
the guy in the photo whom I learned
didn't die, he passed. He was too
young although eternity is such
a long ride we all go too young. But
he was only forty-five, single
and it was a quick-moving cancer
that raced through him like the number 6
Express downtown that didn't stop until
14th Street where he lived. He sounded
like a good man and it was time for me
to leave.

When I walked outside, the heat
hit me as if I owed it back rent
and there was a strong stench
coming from two black trash cans next

to each other looking like lungs after
30 years of chain-smoking. Traffic kept
hitting potholes the size of bathtubs
and I thought about Art for a second
and how at least he was loved. I decided
not to wait for a bus and hailed a cab
to get home to the woman who loves
me, place my arms around her again, with
my hands resting gently on her hips—each
finger a whisper.

Day Dreaming in South Dakota

The night is clear as gin.
The moon hides like a cop
behind the factory that failed
after 20 years like a bad
marriage. The river next to it
turned brown before the first strike.

I sit alone on the west bank
that's too rocky for lovers.
My ancestors were proud
Lakota Sioux and so am I.
Many times I am riding bareback
leading warriors into battle
or buffalo and in every dream
I am chief.

New streetlights shine like war
paint across my face
and a good job could be the feather
that isn't in my cap. I shake
my head in disgust as I stare
at the river no tribe would claim
as their own. It's enough to make me
gulp the last drop of wine I take
from the pint in my hip pocket.
Wine that must be the cheapest
port on the river tonight.

Dumb

When I get down on myself
for not being as smart as the next
guy whose name I still don't
know, I think of John Entwhistle
of The Who, who played bass
like a lead guitar, his fingers
crawling all over the strings
as if it were a spider.

At 56 he was touring and, even though
he had a weak heart, was still
snorting coke. Before a gig in
the Midwest he did a line of coke
as long as a Dickens' novel and
had a heart attack. That was pretty
dumb and I was annoyed
I'd never get to hear him play
live now that he was dead.

Learning Subtraction at St. Mark's Grammar School

The girl who sat in the desk in front of me
had long hair the color of honey that flowed
over her shoulders and down her back.
The day after I dreamed of her, I pulled
on it in math class since nothing there
was adding up for me anyway. I pulled a little
too hard as if it was a rope to a bell I needed
to ring. Instead it made her hand go up
to complain. Our teacher, a Dominican nun,
the Giants could have used on defense to get
into the playoffs, glided quickly down the aisle,
her long rosary hanging from her belt afraid
to let go, each bead a prayer I could have used
before she reached me and told me to stick
out my hand. I looked away as she brought
her ruler down—26 inches of hell slamming
against my open palm. There were more of those
until a month later an older woman with lines
on her face you could diagram sentences on told
us Sister was very sick and would not be back.
That night my mother said *cancer* behind the sign
of the cross and the next day math made more sense.
There were correct answers in multiplication,
addition and for the first time I began to understand
subtraction, now that in a matter of days there
would be one less nun teaching at St. Mark's
Grammar school.

III.

Don't think, dream.

— Richard Bausch

Sidewalks

I don't know how much
there is left for me to take out
of this city. With all the new
buildings, rents keep going up
until there is less sky.
That's why the jet overhead
is the size of a dime and the one
following close behind adds
up to a 25 cent flight out of JFK.
Night hasn't fallen here in years
unless you count the occasional
drunk who falls over and after
he hits the sidewalk it's a safe
bet dawn is close behind.

I thought about moving nearby
but Brooklyn is the shadow I cast
if the sun is at my back and Queens
is too flat without the curves and hills
I liked on those classic Jaguars
then grew to love on Julie London
on the cover photo of her first album.
I might check out Jersey, that is,
as soon as I get my passport renewed.

The guy who lives on the floor above me
is out early. We have a lot in common,
love Sarah Vaughn, Chet Baker and

John Fante. He cross-dresses and I
cross streets. Today he nailed it:
his heels put him over six feet and his
dress and matching lipstick are the color of
Friday night.

We say hello then smile down
at the little girls holding on to a long
rope moving like a caterpillar.
We are both thinking in no time
they will butterfly as their teacher
leads them past the fruit stand
on 88th where the man from Greece
whose English is so broken tape
and glue wouldn't help. Every time
I've stopped to talk we speak
apples and grapes, a language
I can afford rather than understand.

The older woman who lives in
the tenement around the block
from mine is always pleasant but
is angry today and yelling down
at a fire hydrant that seems to be
losing the argument. For a moment
I don't recognize what she is standing
near then remember it's a parking
space. I haven't seen one in this
neighborhood in years and almost
forgot how they look. Before I turn
and head over to the 86th Street subway,

I wish I owned a car for a few
minutes so I could back into
that space just to see what it feels like.

Taking Risks

She sits on the couch with a tissue
in her hand watching the Weather
Channel. I blame her cold on the cold
front they make green on the map
pushing in from Canada. It sweeps
down and curves up like a smile
on a wise guy's face. I hold the nose
spray I brought in from the bathroom
in one hand and a box of tissues in the other.
She says she's fine as I place them next
to her on the round end table that's shaped
like a coin and say I'm going to kick Canada's
ass for bringing cold air into the neighborhood
and messing with my babe. She smiles, thanks
me and reminds me she doesn't want me
fighting anyone no matter how bad her cold
gets and doesn't believe in violence of any kind.
It's just as well since Canada looks pretty
damn big even if I brought New York and most
of Jersey for backup. Then I say I have a wild
idea, let's order a pizza. She looks confused
saying what's so wild about ordering a pizza.
Because this time I say sitting down next
to her, we'll get it with extra sausage. She
thinks for a second, then says let's do it. Life
isn't worth living without taking risks
every once in a while.

Building on Fire

The traffic on Sixth Ave. is heavy
and could stand to lose a few cars.
This section of the city is always
noisy but today the volume is turned
all the way up. I'm waiting on the corner
for the light to change and notice a guy
across the way whose head shines like
the top of the roll-on deodorants displayed
in the CVS window in back of him.
It's hot out which may explain why the suit
he's wearing is the color of a snowstorm.
A large cigar is stuck in the corner of his
mouth and there must be a building on fire
in his chest pushing all the smoke that has no
where else to go out of his mouth.

Missing

I walked home from my friend's
wake on the west side. Tumors ate
just enough of him to make his first
and third wives decide to keep the casket
closed. I'm sure he wasn't in it since
he always said he was going to try
something different, even travel rather
than die. Perhaps on the day the doctors
said he wouldn't make another one,
he got out of bed, snuck past the nurse,
at the front desk, with a hat shaped like a seagull
sitting on her head, hunched over
her phone whispering she needed to be taken care
of for a change and crept out the hospital's
side door. He must have made his way
to Paris by now to drink coffee in one
of those cafés where Hemingway and his pals
hung out or is playing Three-card Monte on
its street corners until eternity runs out of steam.

Black Coffee and Sermons

The doors to St. John's church
are locked every night at 7:00 pm.
A chain droops like a loose belt
across its doors. Even with Jesus
shut-in for the night a few miracles
can take place outside; nothing too big,
the Jets have a two-game winning streak,
a woman with curves like a Coke
bottle may have smiled at you
and not the guy walking nearby,
and every bus you are late for waits
and refuses to leave without you.
The big miracles kick in when the doors
open in the morning.

Inside it's a lot more showbiz
these days. Candles line up along
the walls like the Rockettes in flickering
gold costumes. Sermons every Sunday
are Seinfeld episodes, all repeats
with the jokes you have heard over
and over but still make you laugh.
Saint Michael the Archangel with
his long hair and sword is now
the superhero with a two-picture movie
deal and the voice of God sounds more
like Gregory Peck every visit.

Stop in during the week
when there is no one there except
saints and angels waiting.
You can pray for that three-day
workweek so you can use the left
over 48 hours to feed to your
dog. They may even help you understand
why your smartphone is just average
and the next siren you hear will never
be a guy from Butte Montana who claims
he's your brother even though he
has your nose.

Don't forget to give thanks for
the woman who loves you and hasn't
yet realized her mistake, every film
with De Niro in it, mashed potatoes,
Chet Baker's version of "Look for the Silver
Lining", Keith Richards' guitar lead
in "Sympathy for the Devil". Never stay
too long though, time for these
statues is a cup of black coffee with
refills and they will go on talking
the way only marble can since they
want you to forget you are alone,
lost and on your knees.

The Distance Between Friends

A friend of mine has been saying
for years she had a novel in her
she needed to get out. Last week
she had an emergency operation—
the surgeon couldn't find the novel
or any book and just removed her appendix.

After visiting her, I was walking
home on 3rd and saw a girl
wearing a t-shirt that said *Kiss Me If
You Love To Read*. I hoped she played
it safe and didn't wear it in any libraries.
Who knows what could happen there.
I guess I always played it safe, not taking
chances except for the year I thought
like Vegas and gambled on relationships
and investments. I kept losing and decided
crossing the street was the only gamble
worth taking.

I passed the parking lot on 2nd, heard
kids playing and recognized a friend
whom I hadn't seen in years. He was
imaginary and we did everything together
when we were around five or six. I could see
he was still wearing the same striped polo
shirt and jeans I gave him. I wanted to go
over and say hi but I would have to book

a flight to travel all that distance between
us now.

Across the street from my apartment, a priest
was at the bus stop waiting for the express
uptown. I'd like to think I noticed him because
I've been getting back in touch with my spiritual
side. Although in this heat his black suit and white
collar made him look like a pint of Guinness they
serve at the New Irish pub on 82nd. Each one colder
than the last.

Elephants

I've been living on the top
floor of a five-story walk-up
unless I meet the woman
next door in the hall
who always tacks on a few extra
stories.

The neighborhood keeps
changing. Every tenement
that gets torn down is another
chip knocked off my shoulder.
In their place new buildings
go up filled with chrome and
glass, just thousands of classic
Pontiacs piled on top of each other.

There is one old diner left
where there is always a guy
at the end of the counter staring
into his cup as if he is telling fortunes.
It's still a lot cheaper than the cafés
where they place cream on top
of coffee, piled high as snowdrifts,
costing more than a divorce with exotic
names of places I'd never visit let alone
put in my mouth.

Even the church on Second converted

to some religion more upscale and got
a new coat of paint, cashmere maybe
or the kind found on the racks
in Bloomingdales.

A friend wants me to visit him
in Maine next week. It seems rather far
but not as far as the young woman
standing next to me waiting to cross
the street in a dress that makes
tissue look heavy.

If there was a zoo nearby, it would
explain the two garbage trucks moving

up Third like elephants. And when a police
car siren goes off it makes me jump
and pigeons fly.

How a Black Stone Disappears

We were in Ireland the first
time my dad was back after
leaving when he was a kid, now
with his kids in the back
of a small van. He wanted to show
us where he came from.
We first visited three concrete
walls, all that was left of his
one-room cottage in Galway,
now filled with a goat and most
of July. There was a pub in a village
where his father cursed the English
and drank himself mayor
every night and a river our dad
fished in that hadn't stopped
running and wasn't the least bit tired.

We then drove to the church
that was built when Jesus
was getting big and prayer was new.
And it was the right prayer
or the wrong road that kept Cromwell's
torches away. It was no bigger
than a man's fist who slams
it down on a table to make
a point. Inside it was dark except
for a row of candles next to an
angel who had never flown with

so much stone in its wings.
We walked out onto the grass
that was always wet, convincing
my brothers and I the entire
country was dipped in holy water.

Back in the van, we drove
towards a large green carpet
someone flung buttons on.
When we got closer it became
a field with sheep grazing.
A priest was walking towards us
reading a bible and never looked
up as if he were staring into an iPhone.
He was wearing a black robe and
I thought he must have cut
a piece of sky one night that wasn't
stained with stars
and tied it around his shoulders
like a cape. As we passed,
I turned to watch him walk
until he was a black stone
and disappeared. We were
headed towards Dublin on ancient
roads that would never be that
young again.

Photo of My Grandfather Smoking a Cigar

So I had a grandfather who never
visited us much—my dad didn't want
him to. I came across this old photo
of him in a box after cleaning out my closet.
He's sitting in our backyard, a cigar
in his mouth so he didn't have to talk
to any of us. It's been years but I've memorized
everything he never said. I can see he really
didn't have lips, the way I remembered,
his mouth is just a slash under his nose.
Hair he combed over his bald head hangs down
like a dishrag covering his left ear. We lived
thirty minutes outside of New York City but
when I look over his right shoulder I can make out
Dublin, two dead wives, empty glasses of Guinness,
the wagon he could never stay on and ended up walking
or crawling home most nights. He'd then punch
and kick anything that got in his way: wives, kids,
dogs. If I stare long enough, I can see him puff
on that cigar, smoke flowing out of his mouth straight
from the fire in his stomach, all that way, straight up from hell.

Cool

I'm walking on the Westside
and sweating in the heat, the kind
of heat only NYC can hold onto.
I stop to look at an old photo
of James Dean in the window of a used
bookstore. He is walking towards
the camera in a dark jacket with the collar
turned up, a cigarette stuck in the corner
of his mouth and is squinting through
horn-rimmed glasses. That's what
it would take to cool off, to be Dean
walking in a black and white photo
taken in the 50s when there were
more tenements and rents cost as much
as a sandwich before getting dressed up
in expensive high rises. There weren't
any parking spaces then either,
the curbs are lined with thick round cars
shaped like the biceps on the arms
of weightlifters heading into the gym
across the street. I'm sure it wasn't
easy being the coolest guy in the city
even then with Newman and Brando
around. It looks like it was taken
just before he made it reminding me
of all the jobs I had where I kept trying
to make it. Now all I want to do is just
make it to the corner and head home.

With the blinds closed my studio
looks like a small jazz club, maybe the one
Dean is headed to in that photo.
And with the A/C turned up and
the fan spinning it sounds like a new
tune Ben Webster, in his suit and
fedora, is blowing through his sax.
Maybe it's 1954 or 5 again and I'm resting
on the couch with my eyes closed
listening to him play—every note long,
slow and cool.

Peace Offering

I still don't know what to do
with the jacket hanging in my
closet. It's not that old but like
a Brautigan novel is out of fashion.
Maybe it all comes down to math
and how for the first time in
my life I understand subtraction.
After losing two close friends,
a number that never seemed
large is now a mountain.
Of course raw fish has always
been worth the risk and my last
job offer was not.

The same tall priest in a black
suit I've seen a few times on the street
just passed me again. Perhaps
it is a sign that prayers when
they travel the length of Johnny Cash
will never be answered. On the other
hand this is my fist that looks
like a club and from time to time
I only use it on myself. For my
next trick it is holding a bouquet
of flowers, bright roses since
that is what you are thinking.
Here. They are for you. I'm serious.
Take them. They are all for you. Really.

Weekly Horoscope

I sit on the side of the bed after I wake
and have to think for a few minutes
if I really got hit by a car the day before.
Nothing too big, a Fiat or a Mini Cooper
but big enough to make my body ache.
Everything hurts, even my mouth. I broke
a tooth and after paying the dental bill
I'm broke too. I've spent so much money
at the dentist over the years, I'm sure
I put his son through college and at least
one year of grad school. I look out the window
at the high rise going up at the end
of the block—it's eating the last slice
of sky and the only bit of sunlight
my apartment has left. I can make
out workers who are small enough to fit
in my hand. If I were a different kind
of guy, I'd reach up and grab at least
five and place them in my desk drawer
so I could have quiet instead of toast
with my coffee.

I walk over slowly to the bathroom, turn
on the shower and realize when I open
my eyes the water must be coming from
a reservoir laying out in the sun again to
turn its water so tan. I get out in a hurry,
put on my robe and open the door for the paper

waiting for me like a dog I could never
train like that no matter how much news
I fed him. Perhaps if I threw him some
balls scores as treats I could have gotten
him to sit and roll over.

I open the paper to the Weekly Horoscope.
I see that my ego I lost years ago
made its way down the Dardanelles
and is anchored off the coast of Turkey.
By week's end I can find it when
Mercury is in the 8th House—it will be
in the basement next to an old chair
whose leather is dry and cracked
from all the droughts that rested on it
while waiting for the first rains to return.
With the planets in retrograde there
is a good chance I will fall in love today.
It has nothing to do with the veal parmigiana
at the new Italian restaurant with its long
rope of customers waiting to get in.
All I have to do is go back into the bedroom
where she is sleeping. And that's
exactly what I do—get up, walk over
and slowly open the door.

Paris

I'm walking through every movie,
photo and painting I've ever seen
of this city. Parisians stay thin so
they can walk its narrow streets
and not bump into each other.
Cafés are crowded and I can see
Hemingway in every one, drinking
and arguing with writers I don't
recognize. Wine is like a blue blazer
it goes with everything and most days
the sun is covered in cigarette smoke.
Many of the buildings go back to the
Middle Ages—a '55 Chevy is often
as old as it gets back home.

Along the Seine there are bookstalls
to browse through and the best one is owned
by a guy in a brown coat and leathered
skin making him look like a first edition.
Passing sirens still sound the way
they did when I first heard them
in Ann Frank's diary, even though
it was in Amsterdam and I was in
grammar school in Trenton. And it
is the way they sound in all those WWII
movies when Nazis occupied this city
and their sound even made heroes
like Errol Flynn nervous.

Just across the bridge I can't
believe I'm standing in front of Notre
Dame and staring up at its two
towers. I can see Quasimodo riding
the bells, as if they are giant swans,
making them swing and ring
over the city the way any guy
would with a bad back showing off
in front of the woman he loves.
I then stroll through open markets
in St. Germaine where fruits
are a circus of colors and always
easy to translate, wheels of cheese
cut open to show how deep good
can reach and fish on ice looking
as fresh as a group of spoiled rich kids.

I stop in a church near Luxembourg
Gardens and go over to a corner that
hasn't seen sunlight since Voltaire
and watch candles dance like street
performers then light one instead
of saying a prayer since my French
isn't that good. There is a café nearby
whose name keeps tripping over the letters
in my mouth and just becomes a sound.
After dinner I stand outside under
a moon-shaped like the croissant
I left on my plate. Tomorrow I'll
fly home to my walkup tenement

that looks nothing like these elegant
buildings that resemble Audrey Hepburn.
At least my French will be a little
stronger and help me as I walk
in NYC where on any street if you
close your eyes and listen you can
hear the world.

Playing Poker with Tennessee Williams

The streets are narrow, perfect
for horses or mules, but 300
years ago no one saw cars
coming even if they looked both
ways. Traffic jams and music
are a kind of gumbo. A woman
the size of a parish fills a street
corner with her voice, then plays
her clarinet, each note so sweet
you can drop them in your coffee.
The next song she plays would make
Benny Goodman think about
switching to piano.

Beignets are covered in a snow
storm of powdered sugar that could
cripple the entire Quarter if winter
down here meant what it does back
home. And there is nothing louder than
clothes my cousin wears to parties—
Bourbon Street, night or day, is a thousand
of his Hawaiian shirts.

On St. Peter's Street, I found Tennessee Williams'
building where he rented a top floor
studio and began *Streetcar*. I looked in
at the front stairs where he had Stanley
stand for the first time yelling like an abused

dog just kicked in the stomach up to the woman
he loved who would become Stella
in the next draft.

I'd be the first to admit when
I walked away I moved a little
like Brando before stopping
to watch a parade of school
kids dancing down Royal Street.
A few teachers were playing horns,
banjos and some were moving
umbrellas up and down like pistons
in an engine to keep those kids moving.

I found myself in front of the house
Williams owned according to a plaque
near the door. Across from it was
Marti's Restaurant where he went
every afternoon to drink and play
cards. I stared at the porch where
he sat and watched myself walk over,
asked if I could play, pulled up a chair,
then beat him at poker. Of course
I should have let him win except
I knew it was the only souvenir I would
ever really want to bring home.

KEVIN PILKINGTON is a member of the writing faculty at Sarah Lawrence College. He is the author of nine collections: *Spare Change* was the La Jolla Poets Press National Book Award winner; *Getting By* won the Ledge chapbook award; *In the Eyes of a Dog* received the New York Book Festival Award; *The Unemployed Man Who Became a Tree* was a Milt Kessler Poetry Book Award finalist. His poetry has appeared in many anthologies including: *Birthday Poems: A Celebration*, *Western Wind*, and *Contemporary Poetry of New England*. Over the years, he has been nominated for four Pushcarts. His poems have appeared in numerous magazines including: *The Harvard Review, Poetry, Ploughshares, Iowa Review, Boston Review, Yankee,* etc. He has taught and lectured at numerous colleges and universities including The New School, Manhattanville College, MIT, University of Michigan, Susquehanna University, Georgia Tech. His debut novel *Summer Shares* was published in 2012 and a paperback edition was reissued in summer 2014. His collection *Where You Want To Be: New and Selected Poems* was a 2017 IPPY Award Winner. He recently completed a second novel.